Carolina Wrens

Their Family Story

Story and Photographs by Gail Diederich

With gratitude to
all the little birds
who sing their
hearts out for us.
Gail Diederich

the Peppertree Press

Sarasota, Florida

Appreciation

With appreciation to my first grade teacher, Fannie Mae Arnold,
whose note to me in May 1956 has been a continued inspiration:
"Keep on writing. Who knows, you may be a real story writer someday."

For information regarding permission,
call 941-922-2662 or contact us at our website:
www.peppertreepublishing.com or write to:
the Peppertree Press, LLC.
Attention: Publisher
1269 First Street, Suite 7
Sarasota, Florida 34236

ISBN: 978-1-61493-348-9

Library of Congress Number: 2015903654

Printed April 2015

DEDICATION

This book is dedicated with sincere appreciation to friends and family who are always chief encouragers of my writing. Thanks to my husband Jay for his immense love and support and especially for being excellent as "the grammar police" with my writing!

Special thanks to my friend of more than 25 years, Ardie Christensen Padgett, who is always helpful whether I am asking her to be a second set of eyes for my writing or attending author/signing events with me.

Thanks to my teaching friends from all my years in education. They are always encouraging and interested in what I am writing next. Thanks especially to Donna Benton whom I began teaching with in Greene County, Tennessee, in 1973. Her constant friendship is a treasure unequaled.

My appreciation always goes to my lifelong friend Gail Kelly Lester. No matter what my current project is, Gail is my champion cheerleader. We've traveled many roads together in 65 years and it's always been a joyful journey.

A very special thank you to our close neighbors of nearly 40 years, Harriet and Rene Chavez, who, with many backyard bird feeders, provide a feast for beautiful wild birds that come right over to our yard to splash in the bird baths and often to nest, providing ample opportunities for good photos.

Additional thanks to our across the road neighbors, Roxanne and Paul Gerbase and their children Gabrielle and Dalton, who share our interest in and appreciation for all the wild critters frequently seen in our rural Odessa, Florida neighborhood.

My writing is always for our nine grandchildren: Alysia Diederich; Meaghan and Finn Schlossmacher; Avery, Adelle, and Ruby Kenney and Josephine, Lucy, Maverick Bazin. May these terrific children always find joy, adventure, and learning through reading.

INTRODUCTION

Our world's small creatures do magnificent things that often go unnoticed or take place in spots too isolated to observe. On one rare occasion, events fell into place and we were privileged to watch a Carolina Wren pair build a nest and raise a family a few feet from our kitchen garden window. From first twig in the nest – built in a small clay pot hanging on the wall close to the window - to the last nestling fledging, we saw the story unfold.

The wrens became so familiar to us we gave them names. The male became Enny and the female Essie. Our conversations flowed as though we were discussing family members.

It was a rare opportunity to shoot pictures. I honored the little wrens' space and respected their busy work. They accepted my presence and grew so comfortable with me, as the babies hatched, I was able to perch on a step ladder and photograph the little ones in the tiny clay pot.

Many pictures were taken from the window, about two feet from the nest. Each morning, before the little wrens' activities began, I'd carefully clean the window. Then I'd take my post inside with cameras in hand. It was fascinating to watch them. Sometimes, I almost forgot about taking pictures.

The observation went on for weeks with no two days the same. There was incredible cooperation between the parents as they built their nest. Occasionally, an item was considered and rejected. The male would fly off to retrieve the next item. Both birds were dedicated and worked feverishly as though racing a clock. I came to realize this, indeed, was the case.

When the nest was complete, eggs appeared. First, there was one, then two, three, and finally four. The parent roles were clearly defined. Essie sat on the eggs, leaving only for short periods. Enny would sometimes bring food and gently offer it to her. He was vigilant with his attention to her as she sat on the eggs.

The babies hatched and both bird parents tended the babies with dedication. The care continued until both parents appeared frazzled and tired as the little ones grew larger, gained feathers, and demanded more food.

Along with bringing food, there was the job of "house cleaning", something so intriguing I followed one of the parents to a nearby flower pot to check out the little white glob they took from the nest and discarded there.

A late May morning dawned, and things were very different. The bird parents perched on a swing several feet from the nest. A different chatter was directed to the little ones who understood. It was time to fly and parents were there to encourage and coax.

One by one, the young ones cautiously left the nest, tried their legs, and tested their wings. The parents stayed only a few feet away, urging their little ones to fly. They watched as each offspring succeeded in reaching tree limbs.

It was a touching event. My husband and I stood quietly by the windows watching. We silently cheered each young bird's success, my camera snapping constantly. When the fourth little bird had left the nest and made his way to the tree limb, the parents flew to their youngsters.

Then, we went out and peered into the little pot that, for weeks, had been a flurry of activity. It now seemed very small, quiet and empty. But, overhead, the huge oaks seemed enormously full with the sweet calls of Carolina Wrens.

It was impossible for us to thank the little birds. We felt privileged to have observed this family's love and growth through several weeks. Perhaps a book was a good way to share and honor this very special bird family.

This story, with the narrative supplemented with facts,* is offered with hopes that others will also come to recognize and cherish the very common and very special Carolina Wrens and to recognize the role of all creatures in the wonderful world we share.

*Facts for this book were gathered from sources listed on the Glossary Page at the end of the text.

Enny stood on the deck rail. He was a small bird with shiny cinnamon colored feathers. A thin white stripe above each eye distinguished him from other birds. Enny was a Carolina Wren.

Nearby, a family was celebrating a November birthday. They lingered at the table, talking and laughing.

FACT: Carolina Wrens are common birds found in the eastern United States, south of the Great Lakes and west to Oklahoma. They weigh about 7 ounces and measure about 4 ¾ to 5 ½ inches in length. Males are slightly larger than females. Carolina Wrens are not strong fliers. They move about with short flights, hops, and runs.

Four small clay pots hung on a wall behind the table, outside a kitchen garden window.

"Cheer-cheer-cheer," Enny urgently chattered, eyeing the pots.

No one moved, so Enny tried again, this time louder, "CHEER-CHEER-CHEER!"

Long shadows were falling. Enny was tired and knew night was coming. It was time to roost.

FACT: Carolina Wrens are shy birds but can make loud sounds. Like most birds, they have a call and a song. They utter a loud repeated chattering that sounds like a rising and falling *"cheer."* With their song, it sometimes seems the birds are loudly saying *"teakettle-teakettle"*. Only the male Carolina Wren sings, and his songs are quick whistled notes lasting only a few seconds.

Finally, when his persistent fussing went unnoticed, Enny zoomed quickly, swooped over the table, and dived into one of the pots. He turned his back to the outside, ducked his small head down to his chest, and there he settled quietly. There was no nest. It was just an empty little clay pot with a tiny Carolina Wren ready for a night's rest.

FACT: Carolina Wrens are often seen alone or in pairs. They are diurnal, meaning they are active during daylight hours. They are insectivores and overturn leaves, look under branches, scratch in gutters, and dig into small dark spaces for bugs and worms.

Enny returned for many nights. As dusk settled and the trees grew quiet at day's end, he flew to the same little pot. For a time he sat, always on the same side of the pot, looking out. Then he would turn his back, fluff out his feathers so he looked a little bigger, and tuck his head down. Early each morning, he would fly out of the pot, and he would not return during the day.

Then, one night, he did not return. Days passed and then weeks went by. Finally, month followed month and little Enny was still gone. The pot sat empty until spring.

FACT: Carolina Wrens do not migrate. They are sensitive to cold temperatures. Carolina Wrens' habitats are supported by vegetation like that found in lowland cypress swamps and areas thick with dense bushes. The birds are often found on farmlands, in wooded residential areas, around and in abandoned buildings, and in bushy yards.

April 15

It was twilight. There was a fluttering of wings and familiar chattering. Enny was back, and he had brought with him a mate! They flew into the same pot and sat looking out. Essie was slightly smaller than Enny. It seemed they had decided that the little pot was to be their home. From that point on, it would be Enny and Essie.

FACT: Male and female Carolina Wrens often form a bond and stay together for life. They can be seen moving around their territory looking for food year round.

April 18

For the next few days the two little wrens came at night and settled in the pot. Enny was always on the left and Essie on the right. They turned their little heads inward and hunched their heads down to their chests. Nestled together this way, the little birds, looked like the top of a heart shape.

By early morning, they were gone for the day. Sometimes, one would return sooner than the other and would sit and call for the mate. When both were together, they flew to the pot for the night.

FACT: Wrens spend their entire life in one territory.

April 21

The day dawned bright and beautiful. Enny and Essie were out and about very early. With a flurry of activity, they began bringing all kinds of nesting materials to the little pot. They had slept many nights in the pot with nothing. Suddenly it seemed very important to build a nest.

FACT: Carolina Wrens breed between March and October. Male and female share the work of building a nest.

Different items were considered as nesting materials. Enny would often bring an item, such as a leaf, and perch on the side of the pot. He would wait for Essie to arrive and accept the item. If she thought it suitable, she added it to the nest. If she did not find it acceptable, it was dropped to the deck floor below, and Enny zoomed off to look for the next item.

FACT: The little clay pot measured 3 ¾ inches long by 2 ¼ inches wide and 3 inches deep. It was about 5 feet from the deck floor. The average nest is 3 to 9 inches long, 3 to 6 inches wide, and about 3 to 6 feet from the ground.

Essie seemed to be the "home builder". She would often take a twig or leaf and, head first, shove it into the nest. As each new item was brought by Enny, she would rearrange what was already in the pot. Spanish moss, leaves, twigs, and pieces of string were packed into the nest.

FACT: Nests are usually built of twigs, grasses, weeds, leaves, mosses, pine needles, bits of bark and found objects such as hair, string, and feathers. Carolina Wrens will build homes in many spots including in flower pots, on window ledges, and if a jacket is left hanging, a pocket might become a nest.

Enny and Essie worked feverishly for hours. As fast as Enny could find nest materials and bring them to the pot, Essie would push and tug, working everything into place. A large piece of bark from a sycamore tree was brought. Essie tried to get it in with all the other things. As it dangled out, she'd grab it with her beak and stuff it back into the nest. By late afternoon, it was clear the little pot was filled to the brim. Would there be room for Essie to lay eggs and hatch them in that tiny pot?

FACT: Wrens can build a nest very quickly, or they may take several days to complete it just the way they want it.

April 23

The nest seemed complete. Enny and Essie flew away and did not return that night. A quick peek inside showed their excellent work. They had even found a snake skin and added it to the nest. The tiny nest was perfectly formed and lined with feathers, leaves, and bits of straw. It looked like a comfortable and secure home. The overhanging eaves of the house would provide shelter from rain. The pot was positioned on the wall in such a way it would be very difficult for a predator to raid the nest. It appeared Enny and Essie were smart little wrens who had planned well for their family.

FACT: Carolina Wrens will add a variety of interesting items to their nest. Spider egg sacks have been found in nests and one belief is that the spiders, when hatched, will control mites in the nest. Snake skins are frequently added to nests. It is believed that birds use snakes skins to discourage predators.

April 27

During the next few days, Essie went in and out of the nest frequently. Four days after the nest was complete, there were three tiny eggs.

April 28

On the fifth day after the nest was completed, the fourth and final egg appeared!

FACT: A Carolina Wren female will usually lay 3 to 4 eggs that are light pink or white with tiny brown markings.

April 29

Now it was time for Essie to sit on the eggs. She was warming them and helping the new babies inside grow. She would switch positions, sometimes facing left and other times to the right. She rarely left the nest, but when she did, it was only for short periods of time. She would peer out and watch all that was going on around her. She looked snug and comfortable. Often, Enny would come and sit nearby.

One Sunday afternoon, Enny flew to the nest with a big bug. He perched on the side of the pot and, as Essie opened her mouth, he fed her the treat. It seemed he might be practicing feeding for when the babies hatched.

FACT: The incubation period – the time it takes for the baby wrens to grow inside the egg – is about 12 to 16 days. It's necessary for the eggs to be kept warm and gently turned, allowing for proper development. The mother bird has the job of sitting on the eggs and rarely leaves the nest for this period of time.

May 12

About 7:00 a.m., the first baby wren was out of the shell! The little bird, with huge bulging eyes not yet open, tiny feet, pink skin, and a few wisps of wet feathers on its head, looked helpless.

By noon, a second baby had hatched.

May 13

One day later, all four babies had successfully hatched. The pieces of shell were gone from the nest.

The baby wrens had shiny fuzzy heads, and their eyes were not open or distinct. Their skin was wrinkled and so thin that veins could be seen. The baby wrens' mouths were outlined in yellow, giving them an ever present smiley face. They moved and squirmed around a good bit when Essie was away from them. She spent much time, day and night, sitting on them. They needed her to keep them warm until their feathers grew.

FACT: The baby birds' eyes are closed for about three days after hatching. They have a soft down covering. They are helpless and totally dependent on the mother for warmth and protection. The female stays with the babies day and night for the first four days. After hatching, the egg shells may be eaten by the mother adding nutrition to her diet, or the parents may carry away pieces of the shell, leaving the nest fresh and clean.

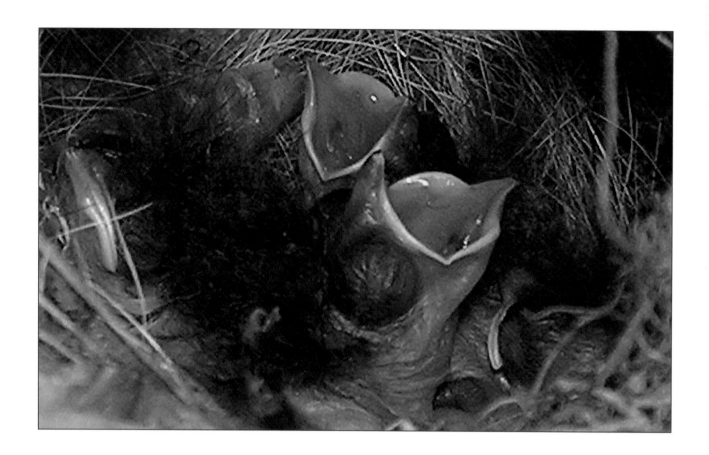

May 14

After the baby wrens hatched, there was much activity in the nest. They seemed to always be hungry. Their mouths appeared unusually large and inside was bright yellow. The mouths made a good target when the parents brought food. Even though they could not see, the babies knew when Essie or Enny had arrived with food. Their mouths quickly popped open.

FACT: The nesting period – the time after hatching – is 10 to 16 days. During this time much growth takes place.

May 15

The little wrens' mouths opened widely at the slightest sound, even a human voice. Enny and Essie made fast trips back and forth all day, bringing small insects to feed their babies. They always seemed to know which baby had been fed last and whose turn it was to get the next bit of food.

While they waited for the next tidbit, their little mouths were closed.

May 16

The little wrens were growing quickly. New feathers could be seen. Wings became distinct with shiny black feathers.

Essie sat with the babies through the first several nights. Once the little ones began to get feathers and were larger, she was gone for the night. When morning came, both parents returned to care for their babies. After eating, the babies would often appear as little sleepy heads.

FACT: After staying with her babies for the first four days after hatching, the mother continues to brood them, staying with them only at night.

May 22

As the babies got bigger and stronger, their heads bounced forward to get food. Enny and Essie kept a steady run, bringing food, all day. At the end of the day, when this picture was taken, the parents often looked tired and frazzled.

FACT: A large part of a Carolina Wren's diet consists of bugs, beetles, grasshoppers, crickets, spiders, ants, and bees. They also eat a few seeds. If a Carolina Wren lives in an area that gets snow and ice, they will depend on bird feeders as a source for food when they can't get bugs and worms from the frozen ground.

Enny and Essie were great housekeepers. Frequently, they carried little white "sacks" from the nest, often to a flower pot, and dropped them.

A closer look showed the "sack" was a container of body wastes from a baby bird. The enclosed waste was removed from the nest so things were kept clean. As the babies grew, the parents carried more and more little "sacks" from the nest.

FACT: A fecal sack is a mucous membrane, usually white with one end dark, containing body waste from baby birds. Bird parents carry it from the nest, keeping the nest clean for the babies.

May 25

Almost two weeks after hatching, the little birds have all their feathers. The characteristic white stripes above the eyes appear. The babies are packed tightly in the nest. Enny and Essie are busy from early morning until evening, rushing hurriedly back and forth carrying worms and bugs to their growing offspring. Some of the nesting material has been pushed out to the edge of the pot. The little birds can be heard chattering when the parents bring food.

FACT: Carolina Wrens have a life span of about six years. They stay in the same general area where they are born. They mature and raise their young in the same area.

May 27

It's fledging day! Four little wrens are packed very tightly in the pot. It seems very crowded and full. Enny and Essie start the day by feeding their young. Then, the parents fly to the other side of the deck and begin a rapid chatter, calling to the little ones. They are telling their young this is the day they will fly! The young birds are ready. It's a big day for parents and the fledglings.

FACT: A young bird that has developed muscles and wings strong enough to fly is a fledgling.

May 27

The first little bird takes a big step out of the nest and grasps the pot. The young bird now has the full set of beautiful Carolina Wren shiny cinnamon colored feathers glistening in the sun for the very first time. His little head is fuzzy. He looks all around at his new world.

With Enny and Essie encouraging, the little fellow jumps, wobbles, and flops to the deck floor. The fledgling bobs up and down, stretches new wings and takes off for the nearby tree. One down, three to go!

May 27

The second little wren, stretches a leg out of the nest to the edge of the pot. The parents chatter nonstop as though they are saying, "You can do it!"

The little wren hesitates, stretches out one wing, then the other. Then, both wings open wide for the first time ever and the little wren flies! The screen door, a few feet away, is a safe place to land and catch a breath. Then the wings spread again and off to the trees the little wren flies. Two down, two to go!

May 27

The third little wren pokes his head out of the nest and then settles back inside. The parents' chatter reaches a high pitch until a little head once again pokes out of the pot. He gingerly tests one foot outside, then the other. It seems to feel okay this time, so he spreads his tiny wings and takes flight, but only to the deck rail. He stops, and for a short time, sits and looks all around, taking in this new world. Enny and Essie continue to encourage. He opens his wings and soars to the tree limb where the other two young birds wait. Three down, one to go.

May 27

One little wren waited patiently as three siblings left the nest. He steps to the side of the pot, briefly looks around and takes a quick soar about three feet down to a table ledge. He curls his little feet around the edge, teeters there for a few seconds, catches his balance, and looks all around with big eyes. With a burst of energy, he takes off for the oak tree to join the other three young wrens. Enny and Essie chatter excitedly, seeing their four young birds have all made it safely to a high limb. The parents take a final look around and fly off to join their youngsters.

FACT: Carolina Wren parents stay with their young, helping to feed and caring for them for about another four weeks after fledging.

Late morning – May 27

When the last little wren had taken to the trees, we went to the deck and peeked inside the little clay pot. For weeks it had been a bustle of activity and was often noisy. It had been packed to the brim with little wrens. Now, it seemed enormously still, incredibly empty, and very silent. We turned to our tree shaded backyard and noticed that our trees, however, were joyfully full of a special Carolina Wren family.

AFTERWORD

Soon after our experience of watching the wonderful Carolina Wren family on our deck, we discovered another pair building a nest in a planter box mounted on the wall of our entry. It was an ideal location in many ways except for a neighborhood cat determined to raid the nest. Being vigilant in an attempt to protect the nesting birds, things finally came to a head one night around midnight.

Following is a story that ran in the *Tampa Bay Times* telling how my husband and I met the challenge and triumphed. The story made its way into newspapers throughout the country and many readers wrote saying they were both intrigued by our actions and happy to know of the success. I share this story in hopes that it might be useful, whether protecting baby birds or in other situations.

CAT IS FOILED

Previously published in the *Tampa Bay Times* (formerly the *St. Petersburg Times*)

By Gail Diederich

Late at night he hides in the bushes outside my front door. I've caught him staring intently from the backside of my car, seemingly angry and ready to have it out with me. So far, I'm winning, my main defense being a roll of aluminum foil.

The "enemy" is my neighbor's cat who's determined to raid a Carolina wren's nest in a wall planter on my front porch. I'm equally determined to stop him.

He succeeded last year. Sadly, I gathered up a pitiful baby bird, wrapped its cold little body in soft flannel, and buried it.

I understand predators and the life cycle and I even like kitties, but laying to rest that little baby bird, I felt really angry toward that cat. Yes, he's a hunter by instinct and is equipped with good jumping legs, sharp claws and teeth but this year those aren't aiming for baby birds while their mother frantically flaps and squawks in distress.

Carolina wrens are a common small brown bird with a distinct white line above each eye. They usually nest in protected spots such as abandoned containers or planter boxes off the ground, secure from rain.

I've watched parents construct a nest, snug, compact and just right for a family. Usually there are four eggs and it takes only a few weeks from nesting to fledging. The parents work feverishly and together coax and encourage until the last little fellow tries new wings and awkwardly, at first, then more skillfully takes to the trees. From first twig to last flutter it's a heartwarming observation.

The wrens returned to the porch wall planter a few weeks back. Opening the door during nest construction, we were bombarded with frustrated chatter as if they just wanted us out of the way. Things settled down and only when I perched on a stool to sneak a peek, did I know the mama was patiently waiting the days until her babies hatched.

A few nights ago, there was a commotion. Plants were flung out of the box and potting soil scattered but the nest with babies was secure. It was close to midnight and off in the bushes lurked the wrong doer – that cat! He'd jumped for the planter box but short sight, lost footing or a frantic mother bird flapping at him, forced a missed target. The next move was mine or I should say "ours" since my husband, not especially fond of cats to begin with, paced back and forth, ready to take on the intruder hand to paw.

Late night is not my best problem solving time but I began to rummage through things hoping for something to secure the nest from the cat and that wouldn't further upset the mother bird.

Aha! A thought struck! When my daughter was pregnant, she was determined to cat-proof things like cradle, infant seat and stroller. She'd heard that aluminum foil might be a deterrent so she covered things with foil and it worked like a charm. Cat steered clear; baby things weren't messed with.

I gathered foil – a large roll of heavy duty extra wide - cut strips and duct taped them gently around the planter. Then Jay and I laid down a foil flooring, in the area the cat would use as his launch to the planter box.

It's been five days now. Baby birds have feathers, their little yellow beaks are prominent and mama bird steadily zooms in with bugs and worms.

Meanwhile, that cat, sits in the bushes, hides underneath shrubs and ventures to the edge of the porch glaring at us. To our knowledge he hasn't set foot on the foil and otherwise isn't close enough for jumping to the nest.

I've searched the internet for "cats and foil" and found interesting ideas but no scientific reason why cats dislike foil but for now it seems to be saving the baby birds. Soon our trees will be a little fuller with new young wrens.

Then we'll see about getting that foil off the front porch!

GLOSSARY

Words appear here as they appear in context order in this story.

Diurnal – Active during daylight hours

Insectivores – Animals, particularly birds, whose diet is largely insects

Migrate – To move from one area to another at specific times

Flutter – Move back and forth rapidly

Flurry -A burst of activity

Feverishly – Doing an activity with great intensity;

Mites – Tiny "bugs", similar to ticks or spiders, that bite and cause irritation

Incubation – The time it takes for young birds to develop in an egg

Dependent – Relying on someone or something else

Brood – Caring for young birds or chicks

Frazzled – Untidy and appearing tired

Life span – Length of life; how long something lives

Fledging – The act of leaving the nest and flying for the first time

Fledgling – a young bird with muscle development strong enough to fly

Gingerly – Very carefully and with caution

Siblings – Brothers and sisters

Bustle – Hurried and continued rushing about

INFORMATION SOURCES

www.allaboutbirds.org/guide/carolina_wren/id (Cornell University)

www.whatbird.com

www.biokids.umich.edu/critters/Thryothorus_ludovicianus/

www.audubon.org/field-guide/bird/carolina-wren

ABOUT THE AUTHOR

Gail Diederich is a Franklin, North Carolina native, a retired Florida elementary school teacher and reading specialist and a retired 10 year staff writer for the *Tampa Bay Times*. She lives in Tampa, Florida, with her husband Jay and their much loved beagle, Eddie.

Gail previously co-authored *Tales of Two Gails* with her lifelong friend Gail Kelly Lester and *Barley, A Possum's Own Story* with Lea Murray.

More information about Gail and her work can be found at www.gailsdiederich.com or by email at gdiederich@gmail.com.

CPSIA information can be obtained
at www.ICGtesting.com
Printed in the USA
LVIC04n0357231015
459118LV00003B/6